Welcome To Marie's World
She's A Big Sister Now

Written by CYNTHIA F. JACKSON

Illustrated by SHAKIRA GAVIN

Edited by ELAYNE WELLS HARMER

Jackson Joy, LLC
Grayson, Georgia

Welcome To Marie's World: She's A Big Sister Now
Text Copyright ©2017 by Jackson Joy, LLC
Illustrations Copyright © 2017 by Jackson Joy, LLC

All rights reserved. No part of this book may be used or reproduced in any manner whatsoever without written permission.
For information address Jackson Joy, LLC
P.O. Box 922, Grayson, Georgia 30017
www.jacksonjoy.org

ISBN 978-0-692-84760-2

Author Contact Info:
info@jacksonjoy.org
www.jacksonjoy.org
Instagram @jacksonjoyinspirations
Facebook @jacksonjoyinspirations

To my wonderful children, Peyton and MJ, thank you for inspiring me. I pray that your loving sibling bond continues to grow stronger each day. To my husband, Marcus, thank you for your unconditional love and support and for blessing me with such a wonderful family.

— Cynthia

Thank you for giving us a chance to be part of your child's education and spiritual growth. Subscribe to our newsletter at **www.jacksonjoy.org** to receive information on specials, additional projects, and upcoming events

Marie skipped down the hallway and quickly peeped into Mark's room. Her heart was filled with happiness as she stared at her baby brother with joy in her eyes.

Smiling from ear to ear, Marie quietly tiptoed toward Mark's crib because she did not want to wake him. She thought he was so small, cute, and cuddly, and could not wait to hold him.

When Mark finally awoke, he was the happiest little baby boy. He smiled all the time. Although he was just a new baby, he was already very special in Marie's eyes.

Marie was super excited to be a big sister. She wanted to help Mommy and Daddy with different household chores throughout the week. On Sunday, she gathered Mark's clothes that needed to be washed, and assisted Daddy in the laundry room. One by one, she handed Mark's onesies, socks, and bibs to Daddy.

On Monday, Marie woke up early and rushed to get dressed. She ran into the kitchen. ***"Mommy, I want to help feed Mark his breakfast!"*** she said with excitement.

As Marie fed Mark oatmeal, food got all over his face and made a big mess! Marie laughed and quickly grabbed a napkin to gently wipe his face.

"It's time to go to school, Marie," Mommy said. *"Get ready to go with Daddy."*

As Marie grabbed her backpack and headed out the door, she turned around and said, *"Bye-bye, little Mark! I'll be right back!"*

On Tuesday, Marie thought it would be fun to teach her little brother his ABCs. She got one of Mark's favorite baby books and sat beside him. Mark sat calmly in his bouncer as Marie read and showed him pictures. *"A is for Apple. B is for banana. And C is for Cupcake!"*

On Wednesday, after Marie finished her homework, she rolled around on the floor with Mark. They played all evening, and the sound of laughter rang throughout the house. She was so excited to play with him, and loved pinching his little cheeks.

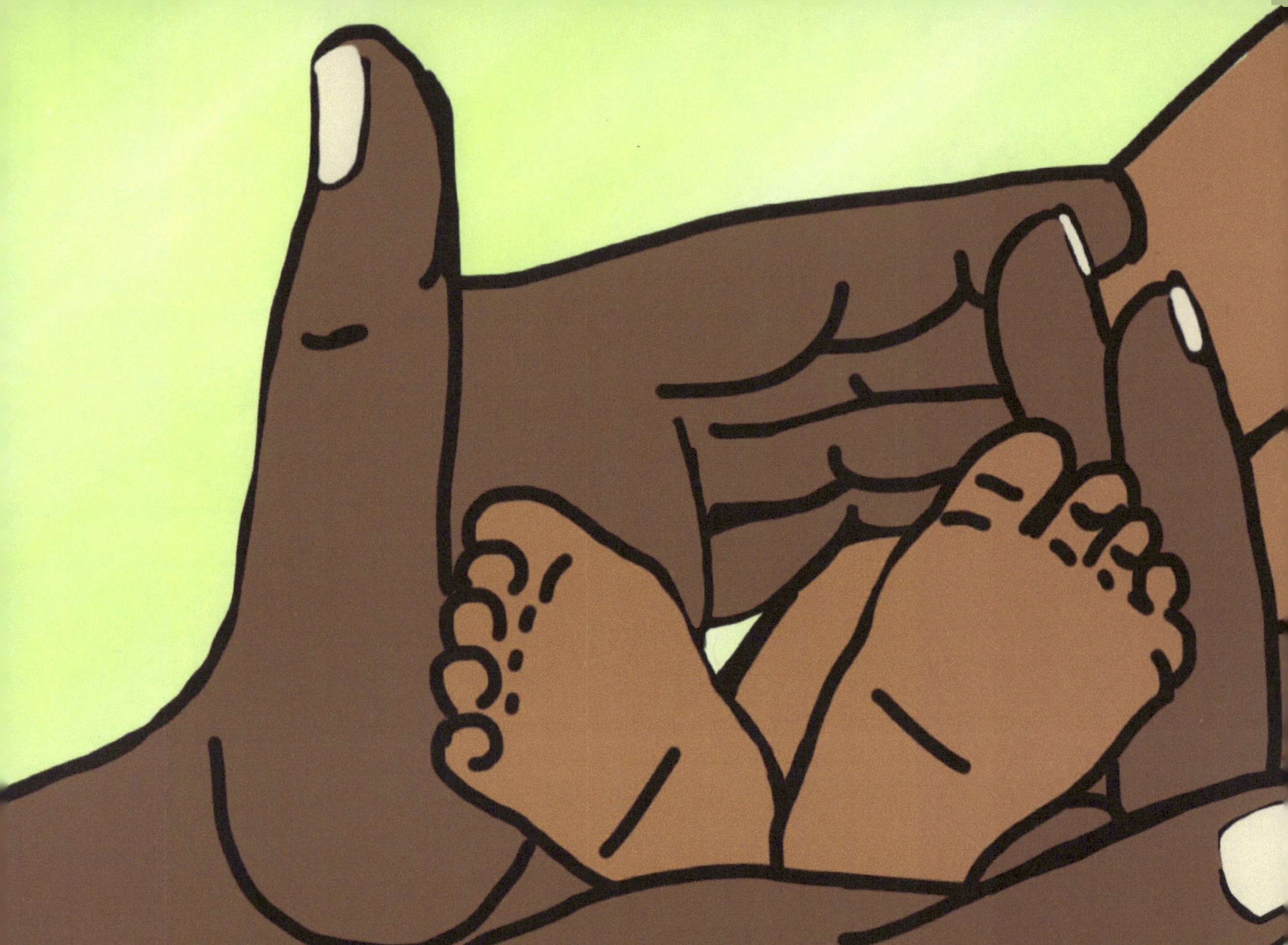

Mark giggled and giggled. He was having so much fun that he fell over from laughter. *"No, no, no!"* squealed Marie. *"You can't get away from me!"* She grabbed Mark's legs and started tickling his little feet.

On Thursday, Marie finished eating dinner and ran into Mark's room. *"I want to hold him, Mommy. Please can I pick him up?"*

"Not right now," Mommy said. *"Daddy is about to give Mark a bath and put him to sleep."*

As Daddy carried Mark into the bathroom, he started crying very loudly. *"Don't cry, baby brother,"* said Marie. ***"Here, Daddy. Put the pacifier in his mouth."*** Daddy put the pacifier in Mark's mouth and he stopped crying.

"What a great job," Daddy said. ***"Thank you for being such a good helper!"***

On Friday, Marie woke up early again to help feed Mark breakfast. This time, Marie was able to feed him rice without making a mess. *"Yay!"* Marie happily said to Mark. *"You ate all your food and didn't get anything on my dress!"*

That evening, Marie wanted to teach Mark how to do gymnastics. She ran into Mark's room yelling, *"It's time to practice!"*

"Look, Mark," she said. *"Put your arms up and jump!"* Mark sat on the floor and put his arms up.

"There you go, Mark!" Marie said. *"Great job, little guy! Fantastic!"*

Saturday was the last day of what seemed like a short week. Marie had been such a good helper all throughout the week. Because she played, fed, and tried to teach Mark how to speak, Mommy took her to the store and rewarded her with some healthy, tasty treats.

Later that day, Mark took a nap, so Marie ran outside to play. She was full of energy and ran around in the grass. *"1, 2, 3!"* Marie said happily. *"Skip, skip, clap, clap!"*

T he time finally came for Marie and Mark to go to bed. *"No, no, Daddy,"* Marie begged. *"I want to stay up and play with Mark instead."* Marie started to cry. She was sad she had to stop playing with Mark, and began wiping tears from her eyes.

Marie walked to Mark's room and watched him as he fell asleep. She stood in the doorway and tried really hard to not make a peep.

As Marie lay in bed, it was hard for her to go to sleep. She kept thinking about all the fun things she did with Mark throughout the week.

She remembered how much fun they had while lying on the floor, helping Mark with tummy time and teaching him how to count to four.

She remembered all the times she helped with naptime, covering him up and giving him a big kiss. Making sure her baby brother was warm and comfortable filled Marie's heart with happiness.

Marie also thought about the many times they went for nice walks outside with Mommy and Daddy, and the time Mark constantly giggled at her when she ran in circles around a tree. She absolutely adored her baby brother and considered him her best friend. Her love for him reached all the way from the grass to the sun and back again.

Marie enjoyed being around Mark every single day. She loved helping and spending time with him as they played.

She thought about him constantly—morning, noon, and night. She felt a very special bond with him and was always right by his side.

She loved Mark so dearly that being away from him made her sad. Whenever they were apart, she never fully understood why they weren't together.

It was time for Marie to close her eyes and get some much-needed rest. Tomorrow brought another day with Mark, and that made her feel very thankful and blessed.

Marie was the best big sister by helping her parents and playing with Mark. She was so close to her little brother, and nothing could tear them apart.

Marie often sang *Jesus Loves Me* before she went to bed. She hoped to share that love with Mark the next morning—the same love that Jesus had for her, Mark, and her mommy and daddy.

www.ingramcontent.com/pod-product-compliance
Lightning Source LLC
Chambersburg PA
CBHW042145290426
44110CB00002B/119